The Underc....

Isle of Wight

A Geographic History

Michael Freeman

ISBN: 978-0-9574514-0-7

Published by Michael Freeman

Produced by: Crossprint, Newport, Isle of Wight, PO30 5GY

Picture opposite: the Undercliff at Rocken End, as engraved by Bradshaw, 1856

Table of Contents

In the Landslip east of Bonchurch, showing the very uneven terrain of the Undercliff here and its sometimes luxuriant vegetation. The steps lead to the Devil's Chimney (author).

Just below the summit of Cripple Path, near Niton, which scales the inland cliff (author)

Preface

This book is largely about the discovery of the Undercliff. If you could travel back in time to the early decades of the eighteenth century, the Undercliff would have been viewed by outsiders as an isolated wilderness. Even the name did not then exist. This did not mean that it was uninhabited, just that it had a very self-contained and self supporting population. The relatively few men and women that lived there eked out an existence from soil and sea. There was limited interaction with other parts of the Island, not least because access to the area by land was difficult. There was perhaps greater contact with other parts of the English mainland coast or with France, for the English Channel was the area's natural highway. From about the middle eighteenth century, however, a steady stream of English 'tourists'[1] began to explore the area that subsequently became known as The Undercliff. A few were island notables, but many were involved in the growing fascination for topographical discovery. In effect, they became part of a British version of the European 'Grand Tour'. Writers and artists quickly alighted upon the area as a key source of creative energy and this soon brought an even wider audience to share in the experience. By the last decades of the eighteenth century, fashionable society was establishing exquisite summer homes in the Undercliff. Some fifty years later, the area was being singled out as a place of winter residence for those suffering from diseases of the chest. And so Ventnor was born as a select winter health resort, eventually acquiring an international clientèle as well as a national hospital. By the later decades of Victoria's reign, wealthy entrepreneurs from Britain and abroad were building mansions in the Undercliff, often for permanent residence. For much of this span of years, the Undercliff remained difficult of access, but all this changed with the opening of the railway to Ventnor in 1866. It not only intensified the popularity and appeal of the Undercliff for rest and recuperation among invalids, but it laid the path for Ventnor's later growth as a summer holiday resort, especially in the twentieth century.

The book offers a geographic history of the Undercliff, an enumeration of key elements in the discovery and development of the Undercliff. It is an exploration in human ecology, an enquiry into the way human populations have interacted with the unique environment of the Undercliff, a feature that remains valid, today, at the beginning of the twenty-first century. The current success of Ventnor Botanic Gardens stems directly from the extraordinary ecological niche that its successive creators have exploited in that part of the Undercliff. Ventnor itself is now on the way to re-inventing its former distinction as an all-year resort, its hotels raising new standards of service, accompanied by increasingly fine fare. In association, food is more and more locally sourced, enhancing not only the Island identity but that of the Undercliff itself. And there is still little that can diminish that first glimpse of the Undercliff as you brest the winding road into Ventnor by the Landslip and suddenly come upon the English Channel stretched out before you. Nor is there much that can take away the arresting shape of Gore Cliff on the horizon as you drive eastward on the Military Road towards Chale and Blackgang on a sunlit afternoon. It beckons to another world.

---

[1] The description is taken from Esther Moir's account: *The Discovery of Britain; the English Tourists, 1540-1840* (1964)

Chapter I

The Undercliff and the Sea

Peter De Wint's watercolour of the western portion of the Undercliff as engraved by W.B.Cooke, circa 1830

The Undercliff hangs precipitately off the Island's high south-eastern downs, a surprisingly narrow ribbon of uneven tableland, roughly seven miles long, elevated at 100 to 200 feet above the sea and for part of its length backed by near vertical scarp faces. Even though we tend to think of the Undercliff primarily as a stretch of land, to appreciate its real character we need also to focus upon the sea, for sea and sky present a perpetually changing medium from which the Undercliff acquires much of its complexion. Sit on the coastal cliff on a still moonlit night and observe the shimmering form that extends reflected across the sea towards your feet. Go back indoors and the reflection shows eerily in uncurtained rooms facing out to sea. By day, on the other hand, there are times when you can barely see much further than your outstretched hand as an all-enveloping sea mist creeps silently up over the Undercliff, coating every object in its path with a thick film of moisture, a fog in which sounds take on a peculiar resonance, for there is virtually no wind to carry them away. Perhaps the rarest feature of the Undercliff is the speed with which its complexion changes. Mists evaporate almost as quickly as they have drifted in and the sun then appears over an increasingly azure sea. In a vigorous south–west or westerly airstream, clouds parade across the wide expanse of the English

Channel like unruly puffballs. In places rainy squalls are visible between shafts of watery sunlight, while brighter skies towards the French coast offer a portent of clearer weather to come. In the meantime, the sea can take on the colour of grey marble, suffusing the land with a non-descript gloom. If the wind is up, foaming wave crests periodically break that marble surface. Towards the shore they seem to develop an almost demonic energy, piling over in a noisy seething froth and then racing up the beaches faster than most men can run. It is perhaps an overstatement to say that the Island's southern coasts can experience weather of all four seasons in a single day. But that is what it sometimes feels like to anyone out in the open air. Nineteenth century visitors never ceased to marvel at the way wild and wet mornings could give way to flawless blue skies and unseasonal warmth. This is what attracted wealthy Victorians to the Undercliff as a place of winter resort. And always it is the vantage of elevation that helps turn the English Channel into an atmospheric diorama.

Looking out to the Channel across Watershoot Bay on a blustery August day (author)

As early as 1790, John Hassell recalled an occasion when he was sitting quietly with fellow travellers near St. Lawrence. Hearing several claps of thunder, the visitors cast their eyes out to sea and observed a small ship labouring under the effects of a highly localized squall. Near the St. Lawrence shore, not a breath of air ruffled the waters, but all around the ship the waves were 'mountains high', the winds 'tempestuous'. Then, to add further to the drama of the scene, shafts of bright light appeared around the 'electric'cloud mass that overlay the ship. Its plight appeared pitiless to the travellers when viewed through a telescope. Eventually, though, the vessel succeeded in making its way towards the shore, away from immediate danger, and the squall seemed to subside almost as rapidly as it had begun. Sidney Dobell, a little known nineteenth-century poet, once remarked on a visit to the Undercliff some fifty years later how disorganized mist-clouds that hung without form and void could be observed furling into form like so many flags at a signal post. From the elevated terraces of the Undercliff, such spectacles took on an added dimension, just as looking *down* upon (not *across*) the sea revealed it as an endlessly reticulated surface, altering under every change of night and day, of light and of shade. Over the nineteenth century, visiting invalids repeatedly remarked how they felt exhilarated by the visible form of the Undercliff's changing airs: it relieved the monotony of physical confinements.

The Undercliff can naturally be approached and viewed from the sea itself. Before roads were improved in the mid-nineteenth century, this was commonly among the principal ways by which travellers reached it. Those on foot or on horseback could negotiate the tumbled and precipitous terrain that lead into the Undercliff from almost every direction, but the entry of wheeled vehicles was hazardous. Even so, the seas off the Undercliff coast were not without their own difficulties, though perhaps not on the scale that characterized the Island's south-west coast, from Blackgang to the Needles, which for centuries had been a graveyard for ships. Between St. Catherine's and Dunnose to the east, tides and submerged reefs may still test all but the best of seamanship. Rocks lie some half mile or so beyond much of the Undercliff shoreline and where tidal streams meet there are turbulent *overfalls*. Here waves can start breaking from all directions. It is no place for an open boat where you may find yourself sliding sideways down the face of a foaming wall of water. The tides here run at four knots an hour, five in springs. If it is blowing hard and you are not in a good sea-boat, the passage can be perilous, as Hassell observed. England's Restoration monarch, Charles II, was caught in just such a sea on 1st July 1675 whilst sailing westward to Yarmouth. He made a forced landing at Puckaster Cove and was royally entertained by the local rector. Coastal pilots across the years have been tireless in their warnings to mariners to be wary of the sudden transitions from deep to shoaling water off these shores. A westerly gale combined with a spring tide can produce breaking waves south-east of St. Catherines's that easily vie with the notorious tidal race off Portland Bill, with its litany of shipwreck tales. As early as 1693, Captain Greenville Collins, rejoicing in the lofty title of hydrographer to the King, warned in his *Great Britain's Coasting Pilot* that mariners should keep their lead at five and twenty or thirty fathoms when in the vicinity of the Island's southern shores, especially at night or in thick weather. A little over 150 years later, the *Pilotage of the British Channel from Scilly to the Downs* still recommended giving the Island a wide berth, for its coast was, generally speaking, 'very foul'.

Given the tumbled and embarried form of the Undercliff, it comes as no surprise to discover that it offers no refuge for ships. In fact, the entire southern coast of Wight is devoid of natural harbours, while most efforts to construct them have ended in failure or, in the case of the modern Ventnor Haven(2003), indifferent results.[1] Local fishermen have for centuries drawn their small boats on to the shingle above the high water line, while at Monk's Bay, near Bonchurch, over the nineteenth century, sailing brigs were sometimes beached to offload cargoes of timber, coal and coke. The off-shore reefs are mostly well-covered at high tide, while in bays like Ventnor, openings were eventually

---

[1] The Haven empties almost completely at low tide and can be used only by small flat-bottom boats. It also regularly fills with seaweed over the summer months.

blasted through them to make for passage at lower states of the tide. Large vessels can naturally drop anchor in the off-shore shoals, but if the wind is rising and the tide running, this always carries risks. Then it is best to sail on for a few hours and find shelter 'inside the island', that is upon its eastern and northern shores.

Puckaster Cove and its fishermen's huts, circa 1830, fishing boats upturned well above the tidemark. The inland cliff wall is clearly visible

In calm and clear weather, the views of the Undercliff from out at sea or along its shores are hard to do justice in words. Over the later eighteenth and nineteenth centuries, travellers never ceased to remark about the painterly images that they saw: views, they claim, that would have idolized a Claude or a Wilson[2]. And, in due course, a string of artists and engravers did find in these perspectives an almost unending source of inspiration. For the Island's leading firm of engravers, the Brannon family, it was the topographical diorama that took pride of place, the successive terraces rising irregularly one upon the other, diversified by hillocks and dells in all shapes and sizes, waterfalls pouring down over rocky outcrops, the whole interspersed with picturesque marine villas, positioned to afford the most capital aspects and views.

---

[2] Claude Lorrain, seventeenth-century French landscape painter; Richard Wilson, eighteenth-century British landscape painter

George Brannon: the Undercliff near St Lawrence, Steephill Castle in centre

For many painters, though, the genre of topographical documentary was somewhat secondary to the qualities of colour, light and shade that the Undercliff unveiled. Whereas Brannon had a tendency to favour facing or only marginally oblique coastal views, painters sought wider perspectives that encompassed land, sea and sky. They looked to explore much more fully the subtleties of the Undercliff's changing complexion. In spring and autumn, for instance, the lower angle of the sun in the hours either side of mid-day can present arresting new images of the Undercliff coast. Buildings on Ventnor's terraces, for example, temporarily acquire a breathtaking, mediterranean-like luminosity. The colours of land and sea momentarily gain a richness that becomes ingrained in memory. Above all it is the quality of light along the Undercliff coast that underpins such visions: the air untainted by dust, coming as it so often does across thousands of miles of open ocean.

Sunset over Ventnor Cove, watercolour by Wm Gray (Senior), circa 1870 (R. McInnes)

At Monks Bay, Bonchurch, *Seaside Cottage* became in the mid-nineteenth century the resort of a wide array of visiting painters. Among them were E.W. Cooke, Myles Birket Foster, Thomas Miles Richardson and Clarkson Stanfield. Cooke was inspired by the fascinating mixture of fishermen's tackle visible on the Undercliff shores: pots, nets, sails, masts and oars. In places, trunks of large trees had been dragged on to the beach to form rough breakwaters from where small boats could be hauled up makeshift wooden slips. Foster was attracted by the children of fisherfolk who played on the shore, presenting them as part of a kind of innocent rural idyll that appealed to many Victorian art collectors. Other painters revealed more fashionable visions: showing groups of finely and colourfully costumed women perambulating along coastal cliff paths. As commercialism began to permeate the artistic profession, wider coastal scenes that could be printed up as post cards became common subjects. Above all, though, it was the seas and the skies that often made for the many artists' exquisite canvases: the gales followed by calms, the constantly changing winds and tides, the gradations of light and darkness, the almost unending ranges of colour. For artists of an impressionist mould, the Undercliff could not have provided a more appropriate environment in which to practise. Some of the Undercliff's permanent residents became generous patrons of the arts, so cementing the inherent attractions of the area as a place of artistic endeavour.

Henry Wimbush's watercolour of Ventnor Bay viewed from Flowers Brook as reproduced for a Raphael Tuck postcard image, circa 1900

Two modern views of the Undercliff west of St. Catherine's, one looking out to sea, the other only a few hundred metres further inland, but set in very uneven ground (author).

Chapter II

Mapping the Undercliff

I am sitting in my study surrounded by sheets of the some of the earlier six-inch to the mile Ordnance Survey maps of the Island. What we know as 'The Undercliff' is covered on three of them. Line them up alongside each other and you obtain a striking impression of the nature of the district. Not only is the eye immediately arrested by the line of the inland cliff face (or scarp) that extends from Blackgang in the west to a point a little east of St. Lawrence Church, but what is equally remarkable is the difference in land use either side of this cliff line. To the north are large fields and open downs, a land of crops and pasture. To the south is a more inhabited coastal strip, often terraced, in places quite well wooded, altogether suggestive of a very different realm.

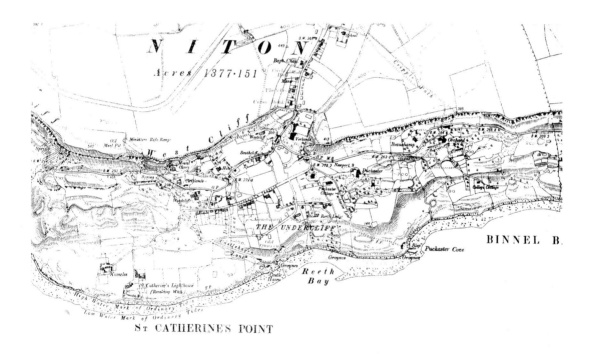

The six-inch Ordnance Survey showing the area of Niton Undercliff – revised in 1938 from the 1909 edition. The differentiation in land use north and south of the inland cliff line is stark

Peer at the map sheets a little more and it becomes quickly apparent that the Undercliff is itself quite plainly differentiated. From Blackgang Chine to St. Catherine's, for example, the unsuspecting eye might be forgiven for thinking that he or she had alighted upon the surface of the moon, for the land appears cratered and pockmarked. There is a disorderly and puzzling array of humps and depressions. Signs of settlement are fewer here and the area is largely devoid of trees. In this portion of the Undercliff, exposure is all. Fierce autumn and winter storms severely stunt most plant growth. Unless in the shelter of very local bluffs, the few shrubs and trees that do gain a foothold become drunkenly mis-shapen.

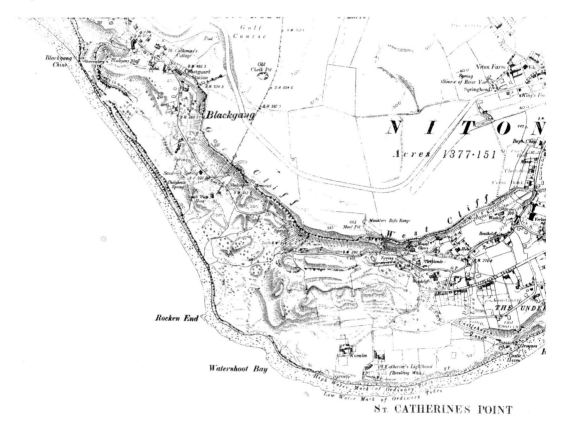

The six-inch Ordnance Survey showing the tumbled terrain of the Undercliff between Blackgang and St. Catherine's - revised in 1938 from the 1909 edition

By contrast, cast the eye across to the eastern end of the Undercliff towards Luccombe, to the area commonly known as the '*Landslip*', and one sees a landscape that is wooded right to the edge of the sea cliffs. The underlying land surface may be as topsy-turvy as the area towards Blackgang and largely devoid of permanent habitation, but sheltered from prevailing south-westerly winds and also by Bonchurch Down to the north-east, it has an extensive tree canopy, as well as a thick understorey. Anyone walking through it on a warm day in summer might be forgiven for thinking that they had wandered off towards some equatorial clime. Naturally the Undercliff figures on other scales of Ordnance Survey map, but it is at the six-inch scale that it is properly able to be grasped in its entirety. It is perhaps unfortunate that this is not the scale that most ordinary map users see it represented.

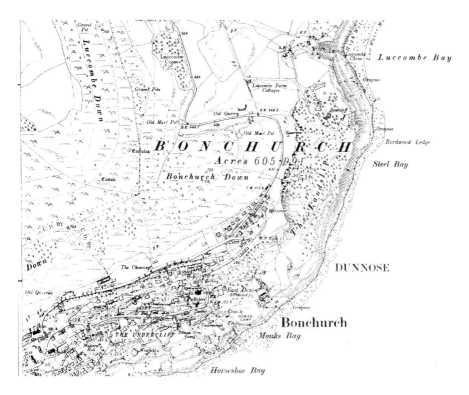

The six-inch Ordnance Survey sheet showing the area known as the Landslip, east of Bonchurch, revised in 1938 from the 1909 edition

One of the paths through the Landslip, east of Bonchurch, as it appears today (author).

The word *undercliff* is first and foremost a geomorphological term, relating to the shape of the land. In the case of the Island, it refers to an elongate stretch of varyingly slumped land, once part of the cliff face proper, that begins at Gore Cliff near Blackgang and continues eastward for about four miles to a little beyond St. Lawrence. Thereafter, the cliff face peters out, but the land to the south of the high downs remains irregularly slumped all the way to Luccombe and, in the case of Ventnor, also extensively terraced. Casting our eyes back to the Ordnance Survey map sheets, however, one quickly observes that the mapmakers of the nineteenth century appear to have had a more restricted view of the area that formed the Undercliff. The name appears in overprinted form to the north of Reeth Bay near Niton, again to the north of Woody Bay near St. Lawrence, and then again at Ventnor. However, it is not overprinted on any part of the '*Landslip*' east of Bonchurch, nor does it appear on the desolate, cratered landscape that runs from Knowles Farm west to Blackgang. What the mapmakers were reflecting was the emergence of the Undercliff less as a unit of geomorphology and more one of human ecology. For here was a narrow coastal strip with a highly sheltered microclimate, offering a choice site for residence, especially in the months from early autumn through to late spring. Even in summer, though, the area proved highly attractive for 'marine residence', its gentle sea airs acting to ameliorate the heat of July and August days. At the end of the eighteenth century, 'Under Cliff' was the name most commonly used for this area. Before that, the land below Niton village had been known as Underwathe or Suthwathe, suth being old English for south. 'Under Cliff' appears printed on Sir Henry Englefield's fine map of the Island that was published to accompany his famous geological and antiquarian treatise of 1815. Within a few years, though, the name had all but disappeared, contracted instead to 'Undercliff' in almost all writings. This was the starting point for the Ordnance Survey.

For all mapmakers, the perennial difficulty with the Undercliff is its instability. The district forms a highly significant coastal landslide complex. In the most dramatic incidents, as in the great fall of 1928, entire sections of the inland cliff or scarp face have given way, generating great tongues of debris that have sometimes extended into the sea. In other incidents, entire sections of land have sunk as whole blocks of the Upper Greensand have slipped at its junction with the blue slipper clay beneath. At the same time, the Undercliff is subject to all the familiar forms of marine coastal erosion. Invariably this acts to exacerbate the tendencies for land movement seaward. This has been especially the case in the area from Blackgang to Knowles Farm, but few parts of the Undercliff have escaped the effects and in recent decades elaborate schemes of coastal protection have been instituted. The task of mapping the Undercliff, then, has had to accommodate a retreating inland cliff face on the one side and a receding coastal cliff on the other. In between, the ever-changing tumbled and contorted terrain has repeatedly tested drafting skills.

To the ordinary eye, the changing form of the Undercliff, as revealed in maps, is not immediately obvious. But what the eye certainly does register is the loss of buildings. At Blackgang, Reeth Bay and Luccombe Bay, for instance, successive maps reveal the destruction to property wrought by landslip events and by shoreline recession. Towards Blackgang both lower and upper roads through the Undercliff succumbed over not much more than 100 years, along with many of the buildings that lay close by them. East of St. Catherine's, at Reeth Bay, a large boarding house and its nearby baths had all too brief an existence, their foundations progressively undercut by storm waves, not helped by very unstable slopes to the rear. At Luccombe Bay, the picturesque groupings of fishermen's huts that so caught the eye of Victorian artists had all but succumbed to landslides by the early twentieth century.

The chronic instabilities of parts of the Undercliff have meant that, in very recent times, it has become more comprehensively mapped in those parts than at any time in its history. But, equally, there were times in the nineteenth century when mapping of portions of the Undercliff intensified. This was where estates were starting to be parcelled up for speculative development. William Spindler's ultimately abortive scheme for a new town three miles west of Ventnor was one example. Another was Dr. Leeson's various speculative building projects in Bonchurch. The maps drawn up in association with such undertakings benefit enormously from the detail that is possible at such large scales of representation.

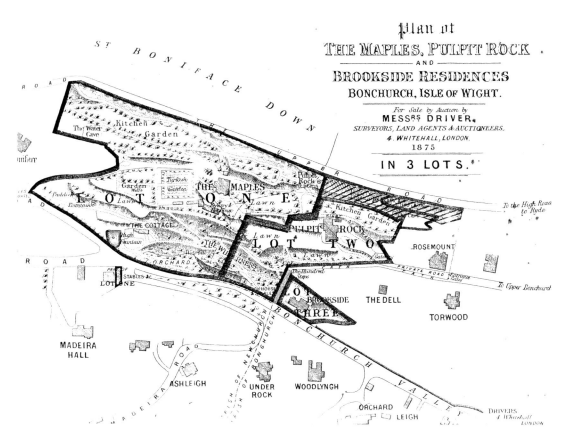

One of many auctioneer's plans showing properties in Bonchurch, 1875

Chapter III

Discovering the Undercliff

For the celebrated seventeenth-century poet, Michael Drayton, Wight held the highest place of all the southern isles, 'jutting out into the sea so far', the 'gentle South' prone to 'court her oft', bathing 'with kisses smooth and soft'. Inland, there were streams and meads to 'furnish every need', while Newport boasted a 'mart' unmatched by any coast. Drayton's almost elysian vision was punctured only by the 'rough ireful tides' that greeted each other in the Solent straits. They roared and charged around this 'bulwark' of England's southern shore. Almost two hundred years later, Jane Austen, in writing her novel *Persuasion*, seemed to echo Drayton's sentiments. Wight was that 'far-famed Isle', easily compared to the coastal resort of Lyme in Dorset where part of her novel is set. The sights and murmurings of shore and sea afforded opportunity to engage in 'unwearied contemplation'. However, by the close of the eighteenth century, this was not wholly the kind of reaction that Wight's southern coasts drew. As increasing numbers of visitors engaged in 'discovering' Britain, the Undercliff among their sites, it was the then novel cult of the sublime that occupied minds. Whilst there were portions of the Undercliff that satisfied prevailing tastes and fashions for the picturesque, it was the simultaneous capacity of the Undercliff to terrify by its cliffs and chasms, and by its tumbled and confused terrain, that appealed to many observers. They saw much of Nature there to be in a ponderous state of ruin.

The Undercliff at Blackgang as depicted by geologist Sir Henry Englefield, 1815 (author)

Topographical writers, artists and print-makers lost no time in 'camping up' such notions, with the result that some of the grand satanic illustration associated with the contemporary re-imagining of Milton's *Paradise Lost* was soon accommodated to the Undercliff. Blackgang, thought by some to be named after a gang of pirates or smugglers that lived there, not surprisingly gained prime position. The size and depth of its chine, bordered by great shelving rock sections, prompted the idea that the earth had just opened its horrid jaws, so John Hassell wrote in 1790. Local springs emitted the smell of sulphur to add to the imagery from hell. When saturated, the famous blue slipper clay had the character of Bunyan's 'slough of despond', ready to sink the unwary explorer. The clay was overlain with vast towering masses of sandstone (the Upper Greensand in the geological column), in places so broken as to resemble ruined fortifications. These extended upward to four or five hundred feet and were piled one upon the other in such a way as to appear ready to fall at any moment. No wonder, then, that travellers of the time described the three-quarters of mile-long chine as a horrible chasm, as arresting a demonstration of sublime scenery as one was likely to find. Some forty or fifty feet above the chine's mouth, a torrent of water cascaded from a black precipice. In strong south-west winds, visitors were struck by the powerful echo that issued from its vicinity. Behind them, meanwhile, the roaring surf offered a reminder of the terrible shipwrecks that attended this coast. In one tempestuous night in the then living memory, no less than fourteen vessels had met destruction in Chale Bay.

George Brannon's subliminal engraving of a stormy scene off Blackgang, 1836

Less than one mile east of Blackgang, at Pitlands Farm, early nineteenth-century visitors could view a rather different evocation of the sublime. Here there was none of the intimidating vertical grandeur of Blackgang, the eye fixing instead upon the great mangled surface, 'black and dreary' according to one commentator, 'nature in her rudest dress' (Bullar 1820). It was hard for poets or painters to do justice to so stupendous a ruin. What had happened at Pitlands is that a large portion of the base of Gore Cliff had, in February 1799, settled and slipped downslope towards the sea. There was no shock of an earthquake, no sudden convulsion, merely a slow, silent settlement. Ultimately more than one hundred acres were affected, the land surface tossed and broken in all directions. A small cottage that had been fitted up to offer refreshment to visitors had been almost completely swallowed up, only its chimney still visible above ground. The overall effect was one of solitude and horror. Nothing animate could be seen at Pitlands any more, save for a solitary sheep picking its way across the ruined landscape and the raucous sounds of crows that continued to inhabit crevices in the face of the cliff.

If Pitlands offered a spectacle of the Undercliff in its rawest incarnation, the lands that extended further east, beyond the village of Niton Undercliff, provided a picture of its mature state. Here the perpendicular, sometime overhanging, cliff wall again takes on the appearance of an ancient fortification. Regular breaks in the rock were described as resembling the shape of gun-ports or embrasures, especially in the hours of twilight. Where the road ran close to the base of the cliff wall, travellers remarked how they felt as if they faced imminent destruction. Everywhere, however, such sensations of terror were mollified by the thick verdure that clothed the terrain around them. Within the shelter of the cliff wall, all manner of trees and shrubs grew in luxuriant profusion. Beneath their canopy, carpets of flowers and bulbs could be seen in spring.

The road through the Undercliff circa 1900, with its overhanging cliff wall, topped by beds of chert. The view today has barely altered. The sign visible is to Cripple Path

Yet still there were the signs that this was a rugged wilderness, a land that had experienced Time's dreadful havoc.The desolations of the past were revealed in huge rock fragments and unexpected hollows and declivities, such that the roadway 'threaded many a devious aisle' according to Gwilliam writing in 1844, an ever winding path into the unknown. Travellers quickly lost any real sense of their destination. The Undercliff became all-enveloping, reviving some of the earlier sensations of terror. Thus the sublime and the picturesque became fused. The Undercliff became both wild and wonderful. One writer remarked that Heaven itself could scarcely be more beautiful, while another described the cliff face as like a wall up into Heaven. It might have been a subject for the painter John Martin, famous for his imaginary scenes from the Bible, awash in the early nineteenth-century's romantic imagination.

At the easternmost part of the Undercliff, beyond Bonchurch, in an area appropriately named East End, early visitors were presented with yet more evocations of the sublime and the picturesque. The towering conical mass of St. Boniface Down to the north-west, almost eight hundred feet in height, reinforced the sense of a wall up to Heaven. Upon its lower slopes, miniature cascades tumbled down in the direction of the Undercliff and the shore. In places, they poured out over sandstone exposures or were dammed up to make pools. East End was itself a vast landslip and there were major convulsions in 1810, 1818 and 1847 to add to the many of earlier centuries. In the 1811 event, a visitor left an account of the devastation just days after its occurrence. Some fifty acres of ground had broken away from the upper cliff. Huge masses of solid rock lay strewn across the lower slopes, interspersed with immense quantities of stones and loose marl. Trees could be seen half buried, streams choked or diverted. Almost the entire terrain became inaccessible for a while.

The tumbled terrain of the Landslip, east of Bonchurch, circa 1900

Not far from the steep shute that descended into Bonchurch, a narrow ravine or cleft had opened up in the freestone blocks in one of the major landslip events. It formed a vertiginous descent into the ruined landscape below. In negotiating it, one's shoulders almost touched the uneven walls. In the dank and shadowy gloom, it became like a journey into the underworld. By the later years of the nineteenth century it had acquired the name 'The Devil's Chimney', a name that remains current today.

Looking up from the base of the Devil's Chimney in 2012 (author).

Over the mid to late nineteenth century, and just into the century following, the central fascination with the Undercliff as unseen *spectacle*, whether in its sublime or picturesque guises, rather faded from central view. Partly this was an outcome of increasing familiarity, but it was also related to more materialistic and capitalistic attitudes to landscape and to land. Among the diminishing band of romantic visionaries, the curse of money descended upon the Undercliff. The area became a playground for the acquisitive landlord, for the rentier class - collections of individuals seeking out independent incomes from ground and building rents. Much of the town of Ventnor was built on the back of such speculation, especially in the wake of the extensive partition and sale of what had become the Hambrough estate in 1828. So rapidly did rentals rise that Ventnor acquired the somewhat dubious label of 'Mayfair by the sea'. In turn, land prices rocketed. Likewise, in 1857, when the Earl of Yarborough decided to dispose of large parts of his estate at St. Lawrence, there was a similar stampede to develop. Whilst the sale advertisement made much of the salubrity of the climate and the picturesque scenery, it added that the estate offered 'a fine field for speculation', with the chance of 'an immense prospective increase in its value'. It became a golden opportunity for Victorian capitalists and builders. The paradox was that, in the headlong rush to develop, the intrinsic instabilities of the Undercliff terrain were more and more lost from view. The very elements that gave rise to the arresting coastal scenery of the Undercliff were conveniently forgotten in the scent of profit. Not only were buildings erected with poor materials and inadequate foundations, they were also put up in some of the riskiest of sites. It was at Blackgang that this feature came to be most forcibly demonstrated. In the first five to six decades of the nineteenth century, elegant villas and lodging houses were erected on the accessible portions of the terraces and promontories around the chine. Some were quite sizeable dwellings, with stables, coach-houses and other 'offices'. There were also farmhouses and farm cottages, for the area, like many parts of the Undercliff, offered good grazing land as well as good tillage. There was even a brickyard with 'excellent clay, sand and water' according to an advertisement in the London *Times* newspaper in September 1852. The excavations involved in all of this construction work, coupled with highly rudimentary modes of drainage ultimately accelerated the natural processes of erosion and ground movement that characterized this especially unstable part of the Undercliff. By the final decade of Victoria's reign, buildings were already being abandoned, and over the following one hundred years the story became one of progressive land failure. In fact, the chine itself, taken over by the Dabell family in 1843 and developed as a tourist attraction, lost much of its dramatic scenic appeal. The great yawning chasm that had so enthralled visitors around 1800 was disappearing.

Elsewhere along the Undercliff, there were also some very early casualties of nineteenth-century speculative building. In Reeth Bay, as previously remarked, a fine lodging house of 40 rooms, the Royal Victoria Hotel, was erected near the edge of the beach sometime in the first decades of the nineteenth century. There were sea-water baths and bathing machines on the shore itself, making what one commentator described as a 'perfect retirement' (Venables, 1860). By 1871, however, the baths seem to have been in ruins as a result of the encroachments of the sea, and the hotel appears to have suffered a similar fate, although perhaps due as much to slippage in the land to its rear. This area of the Undercliff remains unstable today, for an attractive Victorian villa, Reeth Lodge, located higher upslope, suffered serious damage in a landslide of 1994.

At the western end of Ventnor Bay, a series of Victorian structures had also succumbed to slope instability by the middle of the twentieth century. Milanese Villa (later named La Falaise), perched on the end of the Western Cliffs, had to be demolished after decades of suffering structural problems. The same fate befell two attractive hotels at the western end of the Esplanade below. Here the final trigger had been the exceptionally wet October of 1960. In fact, autumn rainfall of that year was the heaviest since records began well over a century before. Today, in 2012, there is a tumbledown Victorian villa (a boarding house once known as Honeythorne) that stands forlorn midway along the Esplanade as a continual reminder of land instability. It is thought that demolishing it will lead to land slippage at the rear; and so it remains, sadly derelict, always a talking point for visitors.

The catastrophic effects of modern land movement on a nineteenth-century Niton villa

Over the course of the second half of the twentieth century, the scientific community greatly augmented its understanding of landslides. One outcome was that the Undercliff was identified officially as among the most serious landslide complexes in the country, especially in the context of it being an area of quite dense settlement. The potential scale of environmental destructions had become rudely apparent once more when on 26th July 1928 a massive cliff fall occurred at Windy Corner, east of Blackgang. It is estimated that some 250,000 tons of rock broke away from the face of Gore Cliff. The fall was accompanied by serious slippage of the land at the cliff's base. The rockfall entirely blocked the Blackgang road that had been opened up less than one hundred years before.

The aftermath of the cliff fall at Windy Corner, 1928

The old Blackgang Road at Windy Corner, late in the nineteenth century, where in 1928, a vast cliff fall was to sever this spectacular scenic route westward.

Ultimately the land that carried the road bed was found to have slipped in a confused mass down towards the sea. Over two years earlier, in January 1926, there had been signs of impending disaster when cracks were noticed a various points along the inland cliff wall. At lower levels, trees were seen to have tilted seaward in places. What had happened then is that a thaw after heavy winter snowfall had lead to an accumulation of excess water in the underlying strata. Temporary streams and waterfalls started appearing almost anywhere. This same phenomenon was observed by Council workmen in January and February 1928, again after snow and heavy rains. Drainage work was at once commenced and the Divisional Engineer from the Ministry of Transport inspected the site in March 1928. It was hoped to be able to save the road. However, an ominous portent was the forced evacuation of two semi-detached houses at nearby Highcliff, further towards Blackgang. The massive fall of 26th July 1928 was witnessed by the Principal of Ventnor College who, along with a German friend who happened to be a geologist, was making an excursion to Blackgang that day. First they heard the sound of falling pebbles. Then larger boulders began breaking away. This was followed by a violent grinding sound as part of the face of Gore Cliff slowly bulged. Eventually the entire mass lurched forward into the valley below in a vast avalanche of disintegrating rock and dust. The pair performed a rapid retreat towards Niton, fearful of further falls elsewhere. The main fall had actually been preceded by a whole series of less serious collapses and the same pattern continued for some weeks after. Equally important was the continual slow movement of the land at the base of the cliff. A reporter for the *Times* newspaper described in September 1928 how some 60 or more acres were slipping slowly seaward. Trees seemed to be constantly changing positions and ground fissures were growing wider and deeper. A few had turned into dangerous chasms, with torrents of swirling water in their depths. From the outset, the landslides had attracted hordes of sightseers. Some were observed taking foolish risks in exploring the sunken ground. There were even boats coming round from Ventnor Bay specifically to view the devastation. Despite fears otherwise, the area of disturbed strata did not appear to be extending further along the Undercliff. Westward towards Blackgang, Southview House, the residence of Sir Frederick Eley, did not appear to be in danger. And the same applied to buildings on the road back towards Niton. There was plainly no possibility of re-building the roadway and so a new road was made in 1933, beginning in Upper Niton and reaching Blackgang by traversing the southern slopes of St. Catherine's Down. It bore little comparison to the scenic drama of the old road, but there was the bonus of a dramatic panorama of the coast from Chale towards Freshwater and the high chalk downs beyond. On a clear and sunny morning, the sight is enough to take your breath away.

As scientific study of land movement in the Undercliff has extended, local authorities have been alerted to the need to find management strategies that reduce the risks of damage, both to property and to infrastructure. One critical element has been a programme of measures to minimize artificial re-charging of water levels. Leaking sewers and water pipes, along with traditional 'soak-away' drains, all add to the landslide hazard. Another vital approach has been coastal stabilization, for this works as a brake or barrier to land movement in the Undercliff under the impetus of gravity. Scientific monitoring has become a key part of such strategies, particularly in the more built-up districts of the Undercliff. Areas of differential risk have been mapped and all development proposals are now examined for their potential impacts on ground stability. The western and eastern ends of the Undercliff remain potentially the most unstable and these areas have generally been excluded from attempts at environmental management. Elsewhere the risks vary on a highly localized basis. For the ordinary resident or visitor, they are most graphically demonstrated in the damage that is periodically sustained to parts of Undercliff Drive. In built-up districts of Ventnor, the signs appear as unexpected humps or depressions in road surfaces, in the worst cases leading to severance of utilities. Many tarmacadam and concrete surfaces show tension cracks. Some householders have been forced to underpin their homes. Others have found that building insurance is virtually unobtainable. However, it remains the case that parts of the built landscape have displayed very little movement over 180 years. It is also true that buildings on one side of a street can show little in the way of ground movement, whereas those opposite display a whole range of symptoms of ground instability.

The Victorians built in the Undercliff in a grand haze of optimism, eager for architectural experimentation, unchallenged by the most difficult of terrain if the views and scenery were unsurpassed, always unboundingly confident in their ventures. Today, prospective property buyers and builders take a much more measured attitude. Most new-builds are rafted. Foundations are deeper. Underlying geology is very carefully evaluated. The appeal of the Undercliff for residence is probably as strong as it ever was, but that is now tempered by a realization that the Undercliff is a product of 'Time's dreadful havoc', as Gwilliam so prophetically remarked in 1843. And it is less geological time than time as equated with successive lives of humans, an altogether lesser scale.

Among the last cottages at Cliff Terrace, Blackgang, now only metres from the cliff edge (author)

Steep Hill (sic), by Tomkins, 1795, a pair of early ' Tourists' taking in the dramatic coastal scenery. The view is highly stylized, but reflects the genre of the period and helps to understand how the Undercliff became so attractive for residence.

Chapter IV

Houses by the Sea

It is hard in the early twenty-first century to think of the Undercliff as a kind of extension of Georgian London or Georgian Bath, but this is precisely what parts of it became towards the close of the eighteenth century and in the earliest decades of the nineteenth. Wealthy members of the gentry and the aristocracy began building summer homes in the Undercliff. This typically followed from extended visits or excursions to the area, taking in its sublime and picturesque scenery which for some had echoes of the Grand European Tour and the contemporary passion for the Mediterranean. One of the first such 'houses by the sea' was Steephill Cottage, erected in the mid-1760s by Sir Hans Stanley, then Governor of the Island. It followed what became popularized as the 'cottage orné style, its thatched roofs and white-washed walls on the face of it conforming to the epitome of rurality. Inside, though, it was all Georgian elegance, or, as William Gilpin somewhat mischievously chose to remark, showed 'everywhere the appendages of a junket and good living'. The thatch, according to Gilpin, made it no more of a cottage than 'ruffles would make a clown of a gentleman'. Hassell, around 1790, had the good fortune to view it when under the ownership of Wilbraham Tollemache, later 5th Earl Dysart. He found exquisite Dutch marine paintings adorning its walls as well as magical landscapes in the fashion of Thomas Gainsborough. A thatched bow window gave views out to the west, while from its descending lawns you could take in the whole range of St. Lawrence on one side and the ocean on the other. Earl Dysart's brigantine yacht could sometimes be seen anchored off the shore, its interiors as tastefully fitted out as the cottage itself.

Steephill Cottage was demolished in 1828 to make way for Steephill Castle, the creation of John Hambrough. However, Stanley's original 'marine villa', for this is what such cottages came to be styled, quickly became a general blueprint for others wanting summer houses in the Undercliff. Over the years from George III's succession to the death of his son, William IV, a whole variety of such villas sprang up along the length of the Undercliff, many exhibiting the most fashionable adornments then in vogue. In due course, they became as much a part of the Undercliff scenery as the Undercliff itself, noticed by almost every topographer and artist, observed as if they were among the most priceless of antiquities. Some of the earliest steel engravings of the Undercliff make no mistake of their importance. They peep out in succession from coastal panoramas, their names and owners identified in the copper plate legends beneath.

Not far from Steephill Cottage, but closer to the sea cliff, was perhaps one of the most famous of the marine villas. It was built in 1794 by Sir Richard Worsley, owner of Appuldurcombe House at nearby Wroxall and a great collector of arts and antiquities. Entrance to 'Sea Cottage', as it was first known, was via a gateway designed by Inigo Jones that had formerly stood at Hampton Court. In the grounds, visitors found a pavilion modelled on the Temple of Minerva in Athens, complete with Athenian frieze. A greenhouse within which orange and lemon trees were kept represented a scaled down version of the Temple of Neptune at Corinth. By the cliff edge was another temple called the Seat of Virgil. The villa itself was built originally as a three-bay classical house, but it was very substantially remodelled in a loosely Tudor style by a later owner, with, for example, barge-boarded two-storey porch and two-storey canted bay window. However, the most startling feature of Worsley's marine seat was a fort on which were mounted six bronze cannon. Reputedly, they were cast from the melted church bells of Nantes, seized during the Revolution. The cannon had originally been mounted on a French privateer that was subsequently captured by the English navy off the Island.

Worsley had planted a vineyard several years prior to the erection of his villa. In time, he had 700 vines, propagated from plants in Brittany, a Breton hired to manage their cultivation. In one part, a series of stone terraces were created, the vines espaliered against each rising face. Unfortunately, the vineyard suffered from the salt-laden winds and prospered only in very favourable autumn seasons. Within a few decades, it was largely abandoned.

Sea Cottage (later known as Marine Villa) and its grounds, engraved by George Brannon, 1835

Sir Richard Worsley died in 1805 and his niece, married to Charles Pelham, later Lord Yarborough, succeeded to the estate. 'Sea Cottage' thenceforward became formally known as 'Marine Villa'. Yarborough himself became commodore of the Royal Yacht Squadron at Cowes and his own yacht could sometimes be seen anchored off the shore. Unlike the Worsleys, however, the Pelham family discouraged ordinary visitors and so the pleasures that earlier travellers had enjoyed from visiting this particular part of the Undercliff were lost. This was possibly because of its rising popularity, for the properties of the picturesque and the sublime hinged in part on their being enjoyed in relative isolation.

To the immediate east of the Worsley villa, was another building, originally known as 'St. Lawrence Cottage' in which Worsley's sister Elizabeth lived at one time. Subsequently, it passed to Captain Dudley Pelham, Charles Pelham's younger brother and it became the nucleus for a new villa known as 'Lisle Combe', completed in the early 1840s. It was constructed to a highly romantic design, including square-sided bays, small oriel windows, a central loggia, as well as numerous gables and elaborately fretted barge boards of varying shapes and sizes.

Westward from St. Lawrence, the Undercliff narrows and the scenery takes on a more dramatic guise. According to Bullar (1820), at one 'finely broken spot, with magnificent masses of rock lying about', was the cottage of 'Mirables'. The artist Thomas Walmsley produced a startlingly subliminal aquatint of the location in 1801, the cottage perched precariously above a series of tumbled rock masses and dramatically overshadowed by the cliff above. It offers a wildly exaggerated picture of the local topographical condition, but the style appealed to contemporary tastes.

Aquatint of Mirables by Thomas Walmsley, 1801(R. McInnes)

Converted from a small farmhouse by George Arnold of Ashby Lodge, Northampton, the cottage of 'Mirables' was described in Albin's *Vectiana* (1811) as in the purest taste of any of its rival cottages, great care having been taken to avoid false or misplaced ornament. George Brannon, in 1837, referred to its 'pleasingly irregular' form, as well as its beautifully planted grounds that descended rapidly to the shoreline. In his engraving published in 1823, the front elevation shows a three-faced projecting wing with deep regency verandah beneath which French windows open on to the lawns. The terrain to the rear and to the sides is revealed as densely planted with trees, a feature that remains today.

Mirables in Brannon's engraving of 1823, a rather more sober artistic rendering

A little further west from 'Mirables' was another striking marine villa, 'The Orchard'. It was built of stone and brick to an irregular plan and had an old Tudor cottage at its core. Brannon's engraving of 1821 shows as its most prominent feature a large first-floor projecting bay with window lights all around and verandah beneath. It was home to Sir Willoughby Gordon, *aide-de-camp* to the Duke of Wellington in the Peninsular War. Like so many others, Gordon came to the Undercliff for his health Subsequently, 'The Orchard' attracted several famous artists (including J.M.W. Turner), for Lady Gordon was an accomplished painter and potter. As at 'Mirables', the gardens of the villa also became widely admired. Extending over some eight acres, they included a series of steep, narrow, walled terraces against which fruit trees grew in great luxuriance, the terraces plainly visible in Brannon's picture. Lady Gordon's mother had earlier acquired an adjoining dwelling known as 'Beauchamp' that was lent out to visitors, even though the rear of the property had been previously damaged by fire.

The Orchard as depicted by Brannon in 1821

The last true example of the *cottage orné* style erected in the Undercliff was 'Puckaster', completed in 1824. A contemporary aquatint depicts a striking semi-circular seaward face, the overhanging thatched roof supported by heavy rustic timbering. Full height ground floor windows opened directly on to a lawned terrace. The dwelling, though, was no diminutive affair, for it extended back some distance and sported three separate banks of chimneys. The grounds descended via steps and terraces to the sea, and, more specifically, to Puckaster Cove, where Charles II famously came ashore in a storm in 1675. The cottage had been built for James Vine, of a wealthy merchant background. It was to a design by Robert Lugar who had published books on villa architecture.

Puckaster Cottage, an aquatint by Robert Lugar, mid-1820s (R. McInnes)

West from Puckaster, you come to Niton Undercliff. Here, on the final stretch of the Undercliff coast to face south-eastward, a further series of summer houses were to be found. Westcliff and Mount Cleeves, both erected in the 1820s, conformed to the pattern of the handsome Georgian marine villa, complete with extensive pleasure grounds. Rock Cottage, later the Royal Sandrock Hotel, was built in 1790, and depicted by Brannon in 1827 with a low but classically symmetrical façade, a central thatched roof, a verandah extending along its entire length upon which climbing plants ran riot. Bullar, in 1820, claimed that it offered 'a finer variety of prospect' than anywhere else in the vicinity. The Duchess of Kent and her daughter, the young Princess Victoria, became regular visitors.

The Royal Sandrock Hotel as engraved by Brannon, 1827

For all their variety, the summer homes erected in the Undercliff over the last decades of the eighteenth century and the first decades of the nineteenth were essentially quite small in scale, even in the instances where they appeared as over-sized cottages. This was unsurprising given that they were often occupied for less half of the year. However, there had long been a history of much more permanent residence in portions of the Undercliff, involving building on a greatly enlarged scale. The village of Bonchurch was far and away the earliest focus of such development. But after 1840 it became commonplace throughout the Undercliff, from Steephill and St Lawrence through to Blackgang. The process accelerated under the impetus of Victorian capitalist speculation. It was reinforced by the rise of the Undercliff as a winter sanatorium, a highly favoured resort of the upper and middle classes in search of health, and especially among consumptives.

Walk eastward down Bonchurch Village Road today, walk past the pond given to the inhabitants by the novelist Henry de Vere Stacpoole, and you soon find yourself in a domaine of high stone walls and tall overhanging trees. Behind them stand elaborate mansions, their heavy gate pillars and ranks of outbuildings offering all the familiar hallmarks of gentlemanly wealth. One is reminded of the gated parks of a suburban Manchester or Leeds where in the middle years of the nineteenth century wealthy merchants and industrialists sought refuge from the dust and dirt of the city and separation from the working classes around them.

East Dene is perhaps Bonchurch's most famous mansion, home to the young Algernon Swinburne. Built originally in the early seventeenth century, it was transformed in the mid-1820s in an irregular Elizabethan style for W.H. Surman who subsequently leased and then sold it to Charles Swinburne who in turn enlarged it eastward. In the1860s, Swinburne sold the property on to his son-in-law, John Snowden Henry, a textile magnate. It was Henry who erected the elaborate coach-house to the westward, its circular medieval style turrets, built in the local sandstone, now an arresting sight in any walk down towards the shore.

East Dene's coachhouse as it appears today (author)

The Maples, Bonchurch, a late 19th century view

One of the most important figures in Bonchurch's Victorian development was Henry Leeson, consultant physician at London's St Thomas's Hospital. He bought up a series of land leases and engaged in a sequence of speculative building. His own house, 'The Maples', was located in grounds that extended from the present main road (sometimes known as the Upper Road) right down to Bonchurch Village Road. A plan from 1875 reveals fountains, lakes, a water cave, a Turkish Garden, a hothouse and a fernery.[1] This was quite aside from the usual adjuncts of kitchen garden, orchard, lawns and paddock. Some commentators viewed Leeson's building speculation as contributing to the appeal and refinement of the village. Others excoriated the 'hand of improvement'. Gwilliam represented his criticism in verse:

'But Fashion now is stealing thro' thy groves,
Tainting by lucid rills and shady lanes,
Plucking thy roses from polluted stems,
And turning all thy lone and quiet paths
Into trim roads and populated ways –
Whilst speculation, rooting up thy elms,
Thy knotted oaks and sun-excluding firs,
Seems bent upon illimitable waste:
For here already are her slaves at work,
Blasting the rocks and tearing up the trees,
Whilst Gibson, anxious to increase his fame,
And add importance to a weighty purse,
Has rais'd a villa of enormous size ....'

---

[1] The plan is reproduced at the end of Chapter Two

George Brannon, the celebrated local engraver and publisher, likewise bemoaned the new villas that seemed little more than retreats of opulence and pomp. One of the most startling enterprises was the making of the tunnel serving Undermount, the home of Sir John Pringle, a railway magnate. It burrowed through a rocky outcrop known as 'Hadfield's Lookout'. The tunnel remains today as a powerful reminder of the wealth that was available to expend here.

Bonchurch and its pond in 1845, before wholesale development of the land around it

Among the many other mansions constructed in Bonchurch over the mid-nineteenth century was Winterbourne. It was home to the Reverend W. Adams. Whether seen from the entrance drive towards the north or from its seaward elevation, it has the appearance of a small country house, complete with attic quarters and other domestic offices. Of Bonchurch's larger houses, it is one of the closest to the shore, a feature that Charles Dickens and his family appreciated when they stayed in the summer of 1849.

Direct and relatively uninterrupted views out to sea are not a feature of many Bonchurch houses. The best that could be said of Dr. Leeson's various speculative constructions was that they enjoyed glimpses of the sea. However, what is now known as Ventnor Towers Hotel, on Madeira Road, although just outside Bonchurch's parish boundary, has probably one of the most panoramic views of the ocean for the area. Although much modified over the twentieth century, at its core is a fine gentleman's seaside residence, as modern visitors soon appreciate.

The opulence and seclusion of Bonchurch's mansions ultimately drew residents from Europe and America Among them was Patrick Henry Griffin, a wealthy entrepreneur from Buffalo, New York. In 1893, he purchased Combe Wood (formerly Upper Mount) as a residence for his wife and four children. Combe Wood was an attractive, stuccoed Regency villa, set in extensive grounds not far past the village pond. Surrounded by high stone walls and screened by exotic plantings, it was a perfect suntrap. One of Griffin's sons, Harry Farrard Griffin, left an account of the family's time at Combe Wood. Bonchurch, he observed, had once been a favoured spot among artists and writers. But by the 1890s this artistic and literary atmosphere was long vanished. Bonchurch had turned into a village of comfortable mansions, all in their own spacious grounds. Even the fishermen seemed to have disappeared, so Harry Griffin wrote. Perhaps they became part of the little army of domestic servants and gardeners that were by then necessary to support so much opulent living. The Griffins bought Combe Wood for £6,000 and spent almost as much again in improving it. The family was served by no fewer than sixteen servants, on the one hand an evocation of its ostensible wealth, but also, too, an indication of the cheapness of labour at that time.

Combe Wood as it appeared early in the 20th century

The transformation of Bonchurch by entrepreneurial wealth in the later nineteenth century was mirrored elsewhere in the Undercliff, especially in and around St. Lawrence, at Niton Undercliff and towards Blackgang. Land that had previously won praise for the elegance of its marine villas, erected with a view to the choicest perspectives of the sea, now became much favoured by men who had made fortunes in industry and trade. Their houses and mansions reflected the contemporary Victorian desire for elaborate ranges of rooms both above and below stairs, a function of the increasingly formalized and divided routines that governed lives. The Twining family, the great producers and importers of tea, bought Wolverton House at St. Lawrence, built originally for a steamship owner from North Shields. Opposite was St Rhadagund's, erected for the McDougal family of flour-making fame. The house had commodious verandahs on its south elevation and a striking viewing tower.

St. Rhadagund's, a 20th century view, tower just visible upper left

Another nearby mansion, a little to the east, was St. Lawrence Hall, built for a naval captain and his family. Designed by local architect Theodore Saunders in the broad style of a French chateau, it was originally known as 'Inglewood'. It was set high in the St. Lawrence Undercliff to give wide views out over the Channel. The mansion rather later became the property of Sir Charles Cayzer, founder of the Clan Line of steamships. The property was eventually passed to his daughter who married Admiral Jellicoe, later Earl Jellicoe, of Jutland fame.

St. Lawrence Hall in the early 20th century

Moving westward once more, the road through the Undercliff was soon flanked by yet more Victorian creations. Among them were Woodcliffe, Rockmount and Rocklands, most of which survive today as holiday apartments. Rocklands was built as the summer home of Richard Barnicott, a West Country manufacturer of woollen cloth. The development of substantial parts of this area of the Undercliff had been made possible by the sale in 1857, in 46 lots, of a large portion of the Earl of Yarborough's estate. A new road was made through the Undercliff as part of the sale along with a carriage drive to the shore at Woody Bay. Here the area's wealthy new incomers enjoyed the benefits of sea bathing, often to the exclusion of the local inhabitants.

One of the strangest developments of the Undercliff at St. Lawrence was the scheme to construct a new coastal town on the Old Park Estate above Binnel Bay. It was the brainchild of William Spindler, a German industrialist. He came to Old Park in 1875, following the death of Sir John Cheape of the East India Service who had become famous for his innovative domestic ideas. Under Cheape's occupancy, the house at Old Park had been extended with a new wing. It was also centrally heated and air-conditioned, while every bathroom was provided with three separate taps: one for hot water, one for cold, and one for rainwater. Spindler came to the area for his health but soon found himself at odds with the local improvement board at Ventnor. He therefore conceived of a plan to create roads, a town and a harbour on his land, the whole linked to Ventnor by a three-mile sea promenade. The scheme got little beyond the building of a sea wall at Binnel Bay, for Spindler died soon after, the wall quickly succumbing to successive winter storms. Only small remnants survive today.

The entrance front to Old Park late in the 19th century

The house at Old Park was built originally for Thomas Hadon who had bought the estate back in 1820. As a wealthy London lawyer, Hadon had set about constructing a large mansion under the supervision of a London contractor. However, the local diarist, Mark Norman, considered the resulting house to be 'a poor little cramped place'. Both Hadon and his wife kept making alterations to the structure, their ideas often so at odds that much money was wasted in constant rounds of re-building. It was in the broad style of a gothic villa, including tracery windows, canted bays and low octagonal tower, all topped by complex slate roofs. In the grounds, a large fish pond was made, a corn mill erected and sea-water baths set up by the shore. However, this was far from the end of the tale. It seems, according to Norman, that the Hadons developed a taste for smuggled liquor. For a while, Old Park became, in the words of Norman, 'a shrine to Bacchus'. Eventually, the inevitable happened: Hadon went bankrupt and the entire estate was sold. The junketings at Old Park must have sat incongruously with the fashionable Georgian society that by then spent their summers along the Undercliff coast. And there was an uncanny echo of such events in the Spindler era, for William's son, Walter, was something of a bohemian and Old Park established a reputation for extravagant house parties, drawing guests from among leading society artists and actors.

Old Park lay adjacent to the Mirables estate, with the elegant marine cottage erected by George Arnold. By the mid-nineteenth century, though, it was home to the Middleton family when it was greatly extended to form a country mansion. This included a polygonal tower under a steep conical roof, giving it the flavour of a French chateau especially when viewed from what is now Undercliffe Drive. It was otherwise in the style of an opulent late-Victorian mansion, with large mullioned windows, following a very common design of the time.

Mirables, the north front, with polygonal tower

Immediately beyond 'Mirables', the most notable home among the Undercliff's Victorian mansions was 'Verlands House', a large marine residence complete with belvedere and enclosed winter garden. The dwelling began as a small building known as 'Rosière Villa'. Later it was acquired by Frédéric Vilmet, the son of George IV's chef, and greatly enlarged. Sadly it was lost to enemy bombing in World War Two. It was favoured by Queen Mary in the interwar years.

From Niton to Blackgang, the terrain was always more difficult and more exposed. Hence the facility for wealthy individuals to buy up extensive acreages and to build upon them was considerably less than further east. One exception was the property known as 'Southlands', located just below the bluff that towered east of the Chine. It came closest to conforming to the pattern of a seaside mansion. Set in pleasure grounds of almost 40 acres, it had extensive reception and bedroom accommodation, as well as all usual domestic offices. It was at various times the marine retreat of Dr. E.B. Pusey, the famous tractarian scholar. In the 1880s, it had a brief existence as a Sanatorium, that is before ground movement began to undermine it. When Pusey lodged there in mid-century, it was in the ownership of a Mr. Johnson of Niton. In later decades, it came up for letting or sale with unerring frequency in the columns of the *Times* newspaper.

No account of the houses of the Undercliff would be complete without reference to Steephill Castle. Amidst all the marine villas and mansions, the castle was a unique creation, a mock medieval fortress amidst late Georgian elegance and Victorian opulence.

William Daniell's depiction of Steep Hill (sic) not long after construction

Its creator was the wealthy John Hambrough who bought up the 1100-acre Steephill estate in 1828. The architect was James Sanderson who had restored Henry VII's chapel in Westminster Abbey. Built of the local sandstone (the Upper Greensand), it had a large square castellated keep, mounted by a narrow circular look-out tower. There was then an octagonal tower to the south-east. For some contemporaries, it did not conform to the most correct of tastes, but there seemed no disagreement as to its qualities of the picturesque, especially when viewed from a distance, whether from land or from sea. Its towers and battlements appeared to float in a canopy of greenery. It represented the essence of the romantically picturesque, easily vying with those magical castles of fairy tale and fable. It was the castle's grounds, though, that won most praise. Sir Joseph Paxton, superintendant of the gardens at Chatsworth, thought it was one of the most beautiful places he had ever visited. The terraced grounds were filled with exotic plantings. There were giant fig trees, one of which measured three and a half feet in circumference a foot from the ground, another trained against a wall that occupied a space of almost fifty feet. There was an orangery with trees imported from France. There were fruit gardens and kitchen gardens of astonishing productivity. Vines grew wild almost everywhere. The garden walks extended to nearly three miles and became a favourite among visitors, including Queen Victoria and other royalty. By the early 1900s, the castle had been acquired by a wealthy American, John Morgan Richards. His fortune came from proprietary medicines and products like toothpaste and hair cream. Internally, Steephill had always conformed to the pattern of the comfortable Victorian mansion, but Richards added to it much in the mould of the tea and flour barons who had already colonized other parts of the Undercliff. Today, sadly, the castle is but a memory. It fell to the demolition contractor in 1964, the entire site (including its wonderful grounds) disappearing under an amorphous array of suburban housing. Only the battlemented entrance gateway remains, together with a few ramparts.

Steephill Castle in its final years before demolition

Chapter V

The Undercliff as Sanatorium

One of the most memorable photographs of the Undercliff is not, as one might anticipate, a portrait of the lines of its coastal cliffs. It is, instead, the spectacle of Ventnor's elegant terraces, rising one upon the other above Ventnor Bay. Taken in the 1890s, it presents a sight that was rare elsewhere in Britain: two, three and even four-storey stone villas packed in regimented horizontal sequence on every available rock ledge, and almost every one of them adorned with verandahs or balconies on each floor. The collective impact was quite startling in terms of the apparent architectural uniformity that it inscribed. It had shades almost of a Bath or a Buxton. However, this was no unified building development in the fashion of a Georgian terrace or Regency crescent. What it illustrated was homage to the winter sun, for Ventnor, as well as the Undercliff generally, was (and still is) a natural solarium in the winter season, that is over the months from October through to March or April. At a latitude of roughly 51 degrees north, the sun describes a low arc across the Undercliff's southern skies during the winter. At such an angle to the earth, it ordinarily delivers little warmth even on the clearest of days. But tilt the earth surface to an angle of 20 to 30 degrees south, buttress it with a protecting wall to the north, and you have a natural solarium. This was the central reason why the Undercliff came to form such attraction as a place of winter retreat for invalids. The eminent physician, James Clark, registered the suitability of the area's winter climate in a book of 1830, and subsequent commentators were soon underpinning his commendation with detailed observations of the Undercliff climate and vegetation. Whereas in the Georgian and Regency eras the Undercliff was most commonly sought out as a place of summer residence, from the 1830s until the First World War it enjoyed a formidable and international repute as a winter sanatorium. Seasoned visitors to the Mediterranean said that it reminded them of the summer air of an evening sail on Lake Como, or an autumn night on the Bay of Naples. Today, in the early 21st century, families and children visiting the Undercliff on a February or a November half-term are still taken aback by the warmth that can sometimes be experienced on its beaches on a sunny day.

Ventnor Cove, circa 1830 (by Thomas Barber), then little more than a fishing hamlet

It was at the tiny fishing settlement of Ventnor Cove that the idea of a winter health resort was born. James Clark regarded Ventnor's shoreline and the rising terraces above it as affording unique potential for those suffering from chronic chest disease, notably phthisis or consumption. His claim was that the site easily vied with established winter resorts like Bournemouth or Torquay. Indeed, he observed that its air was drier, sharper and more bracing. Within a few years of Clark's eulogy, the Undercliff, and Ventnor especially, found itself besieged with invalids in search of rooms or apartments. As demand for accommodation quickly exceeded supply, so the area became ripe for land and building speculation. The celebrated local diarist, Mark Norman, described it as having become another 'El Dorado' when he began work as a mason's labourer in June 1836. Flashy firms and needy adventurers had descended on the nascent resort in droves in anticipation of quick profits. Land prices soared and building plots shrank. Lodging houses were erected a breakneck speed. Jobbing builders had a field day. For a decade and more, Ventnor turned into a construction site. There were quarries everywhere, for the local sandstone that comprised Ventnor's rock terraces was a ready building material. Inevitably, roadways were primitive and many turned into quagmires in wet weather. With so much building work in progress, vegetation became scarce and the expanding settlement began to take on a barren appearance. Bankruptcy among speculators added to the disorder. Even so, land prices and ground rents continued to climb as more and more visitors gathered first-hand experience of the resort's winter sun and air. By far the majority of these were invalids in some form and came from the well-off middle classes, most with independent means.

The arrival of so many visitors seeking improved health brought an influx of surgeons, physicians, apothecaries and chemists. In time, such practitioners became critical to the town's prosperity. Intending visitors were encouraged by local property agents to consult with local physicians before reserving rooms. The variations of altitude on Ventnor's terraces needed to be matched to the constitution of prospective patients. Those in most delicate health were best placed immediately adjacent to or just above the beach where conditions were warmest and most sheltered. Those of stronger dispositions benefited from higher locations where the air was more bracing and where there were more opportunities for venturing out.

Many among the gentry and the expanding middle classes read of Ventnor and the Undercliff's attractions as a winter residence in the pages of London's *Times* newspaper. Henry Wicker, one of the town's best known house agents, regularly advertised there. Every information could be supplied, free of expense, to those desirous of passing the winter at 'so justly celebrated' a resort. In August 1846, the newspaper carried an advertisement for a young widow of delicate health who was desirous of becoming an 'inmate' in a family at Ventnor. In October 1862, invalids were informed of the attractions of spending the winter further along the coast near Niton Undercliff, at the Royal Victoria Baths on the beach at Reeth Bay. This was the boarding establishment that would later be washed away by the sea.

Grenville Cottage, one among many cottages and villas that were crammed on to Ventnor's ascending terraces. Each invariably offered rooms or apartments to rent. The majority (as in this case) provided south-facing rooms with double doors opening on to verandahs

After the railway came to Ventnor in 1866, the attractions of the town as a place of summer resort, as well as in the Undercliff more widely, began to grow. The routine of weekly summer board residence was a facility that proprietors were well placed to supply. However, as Davenport Adams observed in a guide-book of 1882, Ventnor in winter remained 'a chosen spot for the invalid, a refuge from the attacks of the English destroyer, or, at least, a soother of the English disease – consumption'. Likewise, the Island's weekly newspaper, *Vectis*, remarked in an issue of January 1899 how Ventnor in winter remained a town of invalids. The townspeople had acquired a wealth of knowledge for meeting the needs of the sick and the infirm. Bath-chairs, pony traps and every kind of carriage were available for hire. Hot and cold sea water baths were available at various establishments on the shore. Some also offered Cabinet, Turkish, Vapour and Medicated baths, all under medical supervision if needed. The town's shops were more than a match for its well-heeled class of winter visitor. The local newspaper, the *Isle of Wight Mercury,* observed in December 1889 how a walk through the High Street betokened wealth in abundance. The most fastidious appetites were everywhere catered for. Costly gems, rich costumes and furs were on display at every turn. There were shopping outlets from London's fashionable West End. Two hundred foot glass conservatories on St. Boniface Road supplied flowers in abundance. Pheasants, turkeys, geese and every other sort of feathered tribe festooned the windows of the town's butchers. It was no wonder that Ventnor had the distinction of enjoying the best shopping in the entire Island.

The variety and quality of provision shops in Ventnor reflected in one sense the prevailing view among physicians that one of the central treatments of patients affected by the tubercle bacillus was a generous allowance of good food. Weight gain, for instance, was widely viewed as a sign of improvement in a patient's condition and weight was often monitored to what today would be seem quite an absurd degree. Certainly nutrition had the potential to aid the healing of affected tissue, a feature that remains the case even in modern medicine. Alongside diet, though, open air, especially in regions unaffected by pollutants, was also considered an integral part of the treatment regime for consumptive patients. As well as presenting a hostile environment for the survival of the bacillus outside of the human body, it could stimulate the immune system. The ideal patient's room, then, was one with doors that opened out on to a covered verandah, facing the sun, and, in the case of Ventnor and the Undercliff, in sight of sea and with all the benefits of sea air. This is why so many buildings in the Undercliff, and in Ventnor especially, all had verandahs, accessible through French or folding doors. Some patients would even be advised to sleep on these verandahs, protected from rain and wind by a heavy curtain. Although it was not understood at the time, such exposure to cold could help boost the immune system.

An extension of such open air treatment was the practice of making patients engage in graduated forms of exercise. Initially this involved little more than strolling very short distances and on a level. As breathing improved, though, longer and physically more challenging walks could be attempted. The system of terraces that prevailed in Ventnor and the Undercliff made its situation ideal for such a variety of recuperative measures. Karl Marx engaged in exactly such exercising when he convalesced at St Boniface Gardens, on one of Ventnor's higher terraces, during two winters in the early 1880s, not long before his death.

The benefits that the climate of the Undercliff gave to patients with respiratory disease not surprisingly lead physicians to consider the area as a suitable location for establishing a sanatorium, that is an institution dedicated to receiving and treating individuals with chest complaints, especially consumption. In Britain in the mid-1860s, roughly one fifth of adult mortality was accounted for by the disease and sanatoria had already been springing up as an alternative to its treatment in large hospital wards in towns and cities. The first prospectus for what became the Ventnor Hospital for Consumption (and later the Royal National Hospital) was launched in June 1867, the brainchild of Dr. Arthur Hill Hassall, an authority on issues of public health. In 1866, he had fallen ill with pleurisy and after indifferent spells of convalescence in Hastings and in St. Leonard's, he removed to Ventnor where he made much better progress. It was this experience that prompted the proposal for a hospital, built by public subscription and open to patients from all backgrounds and all parts of the country. Much money was raised locally, but funds were also obtained through national campaigns organized in London. The Hospital's promoters were fortunate enough to obtain substantial blocks of land some three quarters of a mile west of Ventnor, towards the village of St. Lawrence. The land lay south of the road through the Undercliff and extended to the low coastal cliffs, affording uninterrupted views out to sea. Construction of the Hospital's buildings proceeded over some three decades. But this was nothing like any conventional hospital, for its buildings were arranged in an almost unbroken line along a roughly east-west axis. There was a central service block and a chapel, but the buildings otherwise comprised ten pairs of three-storey cottages with verandahs on the ground and first floors and balconies on the second.

The hospital cottages (or blocks) viewed from the south

Patients were accommodated in single rooms on the first and second floors, the ground floor set aside for sitting rooms. All of these rooms looked out to sea and, as photographs and postcards were soon to show, they formed a spectacular frontage when viewed from aboard ships, or, obliquely, from further east or west along the Undercliff coast.

Establishing the Hospital on what became known as the 'cottage principle' gave patient's the ambience of a comfortable home, set in an environment where the quality of air and light were second to none. Few but the weakest of new patients failed to be struck by the views out from their bedrooms. For the ones used to crowded urban living, it must have seemed like a taste of paradise, especially when sunshine flooded its south-facing rooms in the winter season.

By the 1930s, aerial photography offered even more striking images of the Hospital's position, the long line of buildings ranged for almost a quarter of a mile along a rock platform, fronted by grounds that extended right to the cliff edge and backed by cliffs and downs that rose to six hundred feet and more.

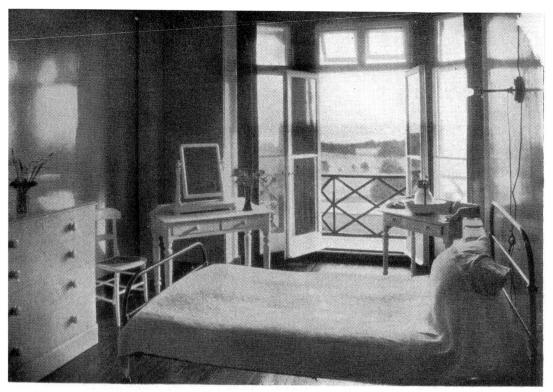

A hospital bedroom bathed in sunlight, its balcony looking south out to sea

A 1930s aerial view of the Royal National Hospital set above the lower cliffs west of Ventnor

One early patient, the 26-year old Thomas Fry, wrote of the institution as being more like a hotel than a hospital, with its tasty meals, its roast beef and marmalade puddings. This was February 1877 when, despite being winter, the weather was warm and sunny. Fry remarked that many patients arrived in quite weak states of health but left quite sound: the place seemed to him to work wonders. However, another patient, Annie Henderson, presented a much sadder story. She arrived at the Hospital in early July 1883 and was immediately placed on the regulation two-hour diet: half a pint of fresh milk at 8, breakfast at 8.30, egg and milk at 11, dinner at one (when she had fowl one day and duck another), beef tea at 3, tea at 5, egg and milk at 7, port wine and biscuits at 8, and beef tea in the middle of the night. Within a few days of arriving, she had been out for over an hour in an invalid's chair drawn by a donkey. Unfortunately, it seems that Mrs. Henderson was already far gone in consumption, for within a fortnight her poor husband was writing to his family that she had died in the early hours of one morning. He had been telegraphed to come to the Hospital to see the last of his poor wife. The contrast was with Thomas Fry who recovered well, married, and then emigrated to Australia in 1881, living until the then ripe age of 65.

Until the coming of antibiotic medicine after World War Two, there remained no cure for consumption, or TB as it was by then commonly known. The Hospital, though, enjoyed considerable success in ameliorating symptoms. In 1901, for instance, 756 patients were discharged, of whom 649 were improved in varying degrees. Only eight had died, with the remaining ones either unchanged or worse. By far the majority of patients were young adults, the cohort of the population most commonly affected by consumption. Generally, the Hospital followed a policy of not accepting patients who were in an advanced state of the disease. For its treatment regime to have real chance of benefit, the disease had to be caught relatively early.

Aside from the intensive nutrition that the Hospital offered, it also placed great store on graduated exercise, following the pattern of the day. By the early 1900s, men, for instance, were allocated one of five grades of work, the lowest involving tasks like collecting vegetables from the kitchen garden, the highest working with fully loaded barrows, for example. Women were assigned similar but lighter tasks, while men and women alike undertook indoor duties such as cleaning and bed-making. Following various land acquisitions, the grounds of the Hospital eventually extended to some 22 acres and, within these, extensive pleasure walks were laid out that became integral to the treatment regime. At the earliest stage of convalescence, patients would walk just for five minutes at a time and then rest. Chairs and seats were strategically placed on paths for the purpose. As lung capacity improved, so the walks became longer, even extending outside the grounds.

Male patients on a work party in the hospital grounds, physician standing on the left

One of the most striking features about the operation of the Hospital was the extent to which the local community of visitors sought to engage with it. They not only supported it with funds but gave time to its patients. Thomas Fry, for instance, recorded in February 1877 how a group of people from the town, aided by a few professionals, were doing a grand performance of Handel's Messiah in the Hospital's Hall one evening. Ticket prices for visitors were from two shillings to five shillings, no mean sums at the time. The proceeds all went to Hospital funds. Fry was struck by how many of the visitors were of a highly fashionable class but nearly all invalids, there to seek refuge in the Undercliff's winter climate. The Ventnor Local Board, in turn, acted to aid prospective Hospital patients by successfully petitioning for an express train service from Ryde specifically for their use. It was inaugurated late in 1891 and continued until the summer of 1898. The journey typically took just 17 or 18 minutes, without intermediate stops. After the service ceased, the practice became to add extra coaches to normal trains. About the same period, the Local Board seems to have adopted *Hygeia*, the Greek Goddess of Health, as the town emblem. Depicting a beautiful young woman drinking from a cup, its *Hygeia* crest began appearing on Ventnor postcards and other memorabilia. Today its most recent incarnation can be found on the side of the sea-front pumping station, the structure built to resemble a large Victorian rotunda.

The Ventnor Hospital for Consumption was not the only sanatorium in the Undercliff, even if it was by far the largest. Church Hill House, in Ventnor, originally a vicarage, took in consumptive patients under the superintendence of a former senior nurse at the Ventnor Hospital. At two hundred feet above sea level, below the Downs, it offered sleeping shelters in the grounds as part of its treatment regime. In Bonchurch, by the turn of the century, there were the Hawthorndene and Leconfield sanatoria which in later years came to be maintained by London County Council as places of convalescence specifically for women. Immediately beneath the Downs in Ventnor, at Huish Terrace, was the Seaside Home for the London City Missionaries, opened in 1867. Although not a sanatorium as such, it nevertheless took in a number of invalid missionaries. On Grove Road, in Ventnor, St. Catherine's Home was opened in 1879 to receive patients in the last stages of consumption. The local newspaper, *Vectis*, described it in 1899 as 'the most charitable of all charitable institutions' – a home where the dying could die. Among its more poignant extensions was a mortuary chapel added in 1892. The Home was overseen by nurses from the Sisterhood of St. Margaret's, an Anglo-Catholic order.

St. Catherine's Home, Grove Road, Ventnor

An altogether different kind of sanatorium was opened on Belle Vue Road in Ventnor in 1903. This was 'Hygeia', an institution dedicated to nerve cases. At 250 feet above sea level, it had uninterrupted views out to sea, and all its principal rooms opening south on to verandahs and balconies. It might easily have been a consumptive hospital. Finally, away from Ventnor and St. Lawrence altogether, there was the Isle of Wight Sanatorium Ltd., at Blackgang. It comprised what had formerly been Southlands, a sizeable mansion situated just below one of the bluffs above the Chine's mouth. It was where Dr. Edward Pusey, the tractarian leader, had convalesced when it was available for rent as a desirable marine residence.

The mansion known as Southlands, at Blackgang, circa 1880

By the time that the company that formed the Isle of Wight Sanatorium had come into being in the early 1880s, the grounds had been extended to 40 acres and a new carriage approach completed. The Sanatorium seems to have been as much an investment venture as a novel health project. Prospective shareholders were tempted by claims of a return on capital of 12 per cent and more. The initial depositors saw their cash used to refurbish the mansion and to construct a new wing. Hot, cold, shower, spray, douche and sitz baths were fitted. Delegations were then invited down from London to view the results, including representatives of the national press. The company boasted an impressive array of medical men on its advisory council. But closer scrutiny of the daily regime for patients reveals the Sanatorium as more a kind of health farm: intended for those desirous of restoring tone to their systems. The prospectus expressly excluded anyone recovering from an illness of an infectious or contagious nature. In the grounds, patients could enjoy archery, lawn tennis, bowls, croquet, quoits and a skittle alley. Pleasure boats could be hired for sailing or fishing. There were also hacks and hunters to be hired. It was, in effect, a rather expensive hotel, but under the gloss of a nineteenth-century health spa. Unfortunately, the venture had a relatively short life. Either the necessary £20,000 of share capital did not materialize or patients did not take up the establishment in anything like the necessary numbers to make the venture profitable. There were also growing issues over land stability. By 1889 a decision had been taken to wind up the company and for the estate to be let or sold. Ultimately, it was to be ground movement that sealed the fate of the Southlands mansion. It was still shown on the 1909 edition of the Six-Inch Ordnance Survey, but it was not long before its buildings were being dismantled, the materials used for construction elsewhere in the south of the Island.

Sanatoria were very much institutions of the Victorian age and of the years leading up to the First World War. They reflected what was regarded as progressive among medical practitioners at the time, but, as always, medical science does not stand still. By the 1920s, they were starting to fall from favour as new treatment regimes were introduced. In parallel, the Undercliff's popularity among the better-off classes as a place of winter resort was waning. The fashionable invalids with their independent means became far less common among the area's visitors, especially as economic depression intensified. Meanwhile the armies of domestic servants that had for so long serviced the vast range of winter accommodations in the Undercliff became much harder to sustain. Live-in service, for example, became not merely much more expensive but less attractive as a form of employment. The smaller of the Undercliff sanatoria were the first to close. Hygeia, in Ventnor, was put up for sale as early as 1922 and became a hotel. The Hawthorndene and Leconfield sanatoria, in Bonchurch, were also later to become hotels. The St. Catherine's Home for those dying of consumption became a school for children with special needs, a purpose that it continues to fulfil today. The Consumption Hospital itself, or RNH (Royal National Hospital), as it had become widely known, came under the umbrella of the National Health Service in 1948. By this time, however, drugs had become available that could eradicate tuberculosis. Surgical intervention had also become more common. The overall result was that the familiar sanatorium treatment of extended rest followed by graduated activity became superfluous. The RNH closed in 1964, its long range of buildings falling to the bulldozer by the close of that decade. However, an element of the Hospital remained: the extensive sheltered grounds in which so many patients had found their way to recovery. These became the Ventnor Botanic Gardens which over subsequent decades were turned by Simon Goodenough and others into a horticultural paradise, supporting over 4,000 different plants and trees, many of them from mediterranean climatic regimes. Just as European visitors once flocked to Ventnor and the Undercliff in the nineteenth century to experience its winter climate, so modern-day Europeans come in similar numbers to see the Island's own version of the famous Tresco gardens in the Isles of Scilly.

Chapter VI

Livelihoods

Before the Undercliff became a favoured summer retreat and then, later, a winter sanatorium, its inhabitants drew their livelihoods from land and sea. Farming and fishing were, for several centuries, primary occupations, invariably geared to the passing of the seasons, for there was a fishing year just as there was a farming year. February marked the start of the prawn season, for example, crab and lobster followed in April, while in summer the major catch was mackerel. Hassell, in 1790, was much struck by the great quantities of crab and lobster that were harvested on the Undercliff's shores. Hundreds of wicker pots or baskets were regularly sunk for the purpose. When not in use, they became as familiar a part of the beach scene as the thatched huts that their fishermen owners inhabited above the tideline. Artists were perpetually fascinated by their shapes and sizes as part of the detritus of the fisherman's craft. One of Ventnor's early residents, Charles Knight, thought that the entire scene could as easily have been arranged purposefully by a painter: for nets, pots, baskets, oars and sails were so carelessly juxtaposed as to be close to the best of marine compositions.

Fishermen and their boats at Wheeler's Bay, near Ventnor, circa 1870

Mark Norman, the local diarist, used to hawk crab and lobster around Ventnor when a young man in the 1830s. It proved rather more lucrative a trade than his work as a mason's labourer, even though there were signs that too many immature specimens were being caught, leading to a decline in stocks. Mackerel fishing was mostly concentrated in Chale Bay, that is to the west of Blackgang. Fishermen from the Undercliff would take their boats round and haul them up upon the beach to wait until the shoaling mackerel were spotted by look-outs posted up on the cliff edge. Seine nets were used to make the catch, the shoal first being loosely encircled and the nets then slowly hauled in towards the shore. In a good year, the mackerel fishery gave temporary employment to a wide range of the local population, for the fish had to be sorted and packed and then carried off to markets on the mainland as well as to island towns. Robert Wheeler, a fisherman from Chale, left a record of how in June 1790 he and fellow fishermen carried upward of 3,000 mackerel in two boats across to Portsmouth where they fetched £1 – 3s – 0d per hundred. Fourteen days later, he records catching another 1,400 fish, most of which were sold locally for 15 shillings per hundred. It was not unusual of an evening to see large numbers of the fish 'playing' in Chale Bay, their silvery outlines shimmering in the low evening light.

Mackerel fishing off Blackgang, circa 1920

Other kinds of fish were also found in the sea off the Undercliff coast. There were turbot, for example. Bass and cod were common, especially in the winter, although the former was not valued in the way it has become so today. Various kinds of shark were seen in the summer season, as was an unusual creature that went by the name of the 'sun-fish'. This was circular in form, with four fins but no obvious tail. It could grow to a very great size, in cases weighing up to several hundred pounds.

The Undercliff fishermen were hearty folk, often with a wild or reckless streak to their characters. Most enjoyed a drink, as did many a fellow inhabitant, made the easier by the trade in contraband liquor that was carried on between the Island's open coasts and France. For most fishermen, it was an easy transition to join the rowing boats (galleys) and sailing wherries that secretly plied to ports on France's channel coast to procure illicit supplies of tea, tobacco, brandy, gin and wine. Any that did not crew the boats helped to bring the illicit cargoes ashore, hiding them or distributing them as conditions allowed. The poet, Sidney Dobell, somewhat mischievously claimed in the early 1860s that the whole population around Niton was involved in smuggling. Everyone had an ostensible occupation, but nobody got his money by it. So there were fishermen who never fished and farmers who 'ploughed the deep'. He went on to quip that there was hardly a man known by his lawful surname. By the time he was writing, smuggling activity on the coast was actually well past its peak, for the Revenue Service was by then much more efficient and more organized in the business of detection. What Dobell was recording was the scale of smuggling between fifty and a hundred years before. It was a practice that was grounded in custom, an activity woven into livelihoods, not generally viewed as anything illegal, merely a vital means of supplementing otherwise unreliable incomes. It is true that a few individuals made small fortunes from smuggling, those who organized the trade from behind a façade of respectability and who relied on a small cohort of trusted servants and retainers to transact the business. Mark Norman recalled one of these leading figures in the trade to be 'as much unlike the general description of a smuggler as possible'. He dressed in the manner of a gentleman farmer: a velveteen shooting coat and waistcoat, fancy trousers, wellington boots and a white hat. The man in question was Ralph Stone, locally known as the 'Great Smuggler'. It was said that his manner was so quiet and his conversation so easy that he always seemed able to disarm suspicion.

It was the smuggling of spirits that brought in the biggest profits. Wherries of between 10 and 50 tons, the smaller ones half-decked, could stow up to 200 or more kegs in their holds, while rowing boats (galleys) could carry up to 50. Whatever the vessel used, four-gallon kegs or tubs would on occasion be lashed to an outboard warp that ran all the way round a boat's gunwhale. To these were attached stone weights and cork floats so that, in the event of a Revenue cutter or gun brig appearing when near to the shore, the kegs could be quickly jettisoned to the sea bed, to be recovered another day, although probably only if sea conditions remained relatively calm in the interim. The Undercliff coast between St. Catherine's and Luccombe was ideal for the landing of illicit cargoes for there was no end of secluded coves where small boats could be beached and off-loaded, or, in the case of the larger vessels, anchored just offshore and the cargo floated in to waiting hands. Although the coastal cliffs could make for difficulties in transferring the cargo inland, the tumbled nature of the Undercliff terrain, the rocky outcrops and the thick vegetation, offered almost endless possibilities for concealment. In places, caves were used to store goods, while in some dwellings there were secret cellars where spoils could be temporarily stowed. Binnel Bay, just west of St. Lawrence, was a location especially favoured by local men, for a secret underground passage ran from the shore to the upper cliffs, opening out in thick undergrowth. By this means, incoming cargoes could be run to ground in very short time. Luccombe Chine, at the eastern most end of the Undercliff, was another common landing site. It was home to a well-known family of smugglers, the Kingswells, who contrived various means of concealment, often very necessary given the steepness of the local cliffs, making distribution of kegs a slow and arduous business.

Smugglers bringing kegs of liquor ashore at Blackgang in an early 19th century engraving

At one time in the eighteenth century, according to Mark Norman, another means of acquiring duty-free goods was to intercept (peacefully) homeward-bound ships in the English Channel. Captains and crew of such inbound vessels could gain significantly from trading of this sort, for it was not hard for ships' captains to claim to brokers and merchants that the missing goods had been damaged by storms. Landing such contraband on the Undercliff shores remained hazardous, of course, and Revenue men were always on the watch for local fishing boats that appeared to be steering courses that suggested a purpose other than fishing. The parish clerk of St. Lawrence, John Green, writing in 1847, also recorded how Irish wherries and vessels from Holland called Dutch Doggers used to come to the Undercliff coast laden with smuggled goods. The Irish boats always came very well-manned so that they could see off any Revenue boats, even to the extent of seizing their crews while goods were landed. The trade in contraband in these cases was not wholly one way, for Isle of Wight wool, the export of which was prohibited, was sometimes exchanged for smuggled spirits.

If caught, the penalties for smuggling, once convicted, could be quite harsh. In the eighteenth century, an able bodied seaman could end up committed to serving five years on a 'man-of-war' in the English navy. Many culprits were sent to trial in Portsmouth.

However, at the Isle of Wight County Sessions in October 1852, three men got away with just six months hard labour in Winchester's House of Correction. They had been intercepted by a Revenue cutter about 20 miles off St. Catherine's and been observed to throw tubs overboard as soon as they recognized they were being pursued. One of the tubs was retrieved by an officer and found to contain brandy. When the fleeing vessel was eventually boarded, a fishing smack of some 15 tons, the hold was found reeking of strong spirits.

There was no Revenue station on the Undercliff coast until 1818. In that year, five officers were despatched to St. Lawrence, lodging in an old cottage there. Subsequently, a watch house was built close to the shore at Orchard Bay. The watch house was re-sited further west at Woody Bay in 1855. The practice of having officers regularly on duty along the cliffs almost certainly helps to account for the falling off in smuggling after that date which Mark Norman recalled when a young man in the 1830s. Whilst crews could, by virtue of superb seamanship, often outrun or evade the cutters and gun brigs of the Revenue service out in the Channel, it was more difficult to outwit a determined group of officers on land, especially where they acquired a close knowledge of the territory and were able to recruit local informers. Smuggling did not disappear, of course, but subsequent reductions in excise duties increasingly helped to diminish its appeal.

Some of those involved in the contraband trade were, as Dobell observed, farmers or farm labourers of one form or another. One late eighteenth-century visitor to the Undercliff, whilst enthralling at Nature's majestic ruins, was quick also to remark that every spot that could bear the impression of the plough was well cultivated and, moreover, proved uncommonly fertile. Everywhere, he observed, were to be found productive enclosures. Even in a number of areas subject to land movement, it was rarely long before small level areas were sown with grain, quickly exceeding all expectations of productivity. The high grain prices that prevailed during the Napoleonic Wars helped to fuel such farming practice. At the same time, increasing numbers of visitors to the Undercliff, especially after 1830, resulted in a steadily rising demand for fresh foodstuffs like milk, butter, cheese, bacon and market garden produce.

In medieval times, much of the Undercliff had been utilized only for hunting, but from the sixteenth century onwards, a host of small farms grew up along its length. When John Hambrough purchased the Steephill estate in 1828, it consisted of two farms: Steeple of 121 acres, and Cook's of 23 acres. Further east, Ventnor Farm ran to some 170 acres and Littletown Farm to almost 200 acres. Here were the lands on which much of the resort of Ventnor was eventually built. It was no idle observation when some of its early residents complained that some of the town's streets ended abruptly in ploughed fields. Ventnor even had its own corn mill, located just above where the Winter Gardens building now stands. The mill pond was fed by streams from above Spring Hill, beneath the chalk downs. Below the mill, there was a waterfall down to the shore, a feature that invariably drew the notice of visitors. Bonchurch was made up of three separate farms, the largest (154 acres) known as Bonchurch Farm, the smallest (31 acres) known as Marepool. It was on some of the fields of these two farms that many of Bonchurch's various mansions were built. In fact, Marepool was to become almost entirely occupied by such dwellings.

Puckwell Farm's rickyard, close to the centre of Niton, early in the 20th Century

At the western end of the Undercliff, Niton had no less than 12 separate farms in 1801, comprising 1,350 acres in total. The soil, a rich loam, was especially suited to grain production. Adjoining it, in St. Lawrence, to the east, were Home and Bank End farms. It was on some of the fields belonging to these farms that speculative building occurred over the nineteenth century, much as at Bonchurch. Even so, despite the many encroachments on farmland that such changes represented, small herds of Alderney and Red Devon cows continued to be reared for milk and butter, for example, while pigs were widely kept for bacon and chickens for eggs. Throughout the Undercliff, the daily milk rounds were invariably undertaken by local farmers, the milk supplied in individual cans. What was left over was put into pans at the dairy to set for cream and for butter.

George Coleman, from Home Farm, St. Lawrence, on his milk round in the mid-1920s

Most cottages in the Undercliff had their allotment gardens in which vegetables and fruit were cultivated and any surplus produce found a ready market among the villas and lodging houses that were springing up in the Undercliff, especially in Ventnor. Even within Ventnor itself, despite the density of building, there were areas of open ground, including immediately above the Esplanade, where nineteenth-century photographs reveal regimented lines of kitchen garden crops in summer. Several of the larger hotels even maintained their own kitchen gardens: that belonging to the Royal Marine, on Belgrave Road, was located in what is now the Grove car park. Much of the south side of Spring Hill in Ventnor consisted of market gardens, including orchards and a watercress bed that was fed by a chalk stream.

From the late eighteenth century, the range of livelihoods in the Undercliff was augmented by visitors in other ways, too. It was not merely that they brought rising demands for food that benefited the district's fishing and farming. What they also required were growing numbers of 'domestics', that is indoor and outdoor servants - cooks and housemaids in one sphere, coachmen and stable lads in another. Then, as hotels and boarding houses expanded over the nineteenth century, in Ventnor especially, there were openings for such occupations as waiters, pages, booking clerks and porters.

The various social elites that built summer residences in the Undercliff invariably provided quarters for their servants or retainers, and especially for the gardeners who tended the extensive pleasure grounds that came to form such a distinctive feature of the Undercliff's various marine villas. By the mid-nineteenth century, as we have seen, new-found Victorian wealth saw the building of large numbers of mansions in areas like Bonchurch, St Lawrence and Niton Undercliff. Together they formed a whole new recruiting ground for local labour – from scullery maids to lady's maids, and from footmen to house butlers. The complex hierarchy of Victorian domestic service was mirrored, of course, by the quarters in which they lived: typically warrens of attic and basement rooms that were in some ways as carefully planned out as the grand reception rooms that their occupants ultimately served. One founding member of Niton's Women's Institute recalled being entertained as a child at one such house following chapel one Sunday evening. Her father was gardener at the house known as 'Windcliffe', near St. Catherine's, and she described sitting down to supper in a huge kitchen with the cook presiding at the end of a long table, 'stately and dignified in black silk and lace', the under servants all around.

It was in the resort of Ventnor itself, of course, that demands upon the local labour market grew most rapidly, especially over the decades from 1840 to 1900, the period when the town developed an international reputation as a place of winter retreat for invalids, and, later, also as a beach resort in summer. The pages of the census enumerators books for Ventnor for 1901 cast a fascinating light on parts of this story. At the Royal Marine Hotel on Belgrave Road, Ventnor-born Florence Vince was a 23-year old chambermaid, Leslie Hatcher, also Ventnor-born, an 18-year old waiter. Fraser Moses, from Wroxall, had a post as hotel porter, while Lilian Ribbands, from Bonchurch, was a clerk there. All of these individuals were 'live-in' servants and there would have been many others from Ventnor and its surrounding villages who lived out. It is clear, too, that people came to Ventnor from the mainland and from Ireland in search of employment. Clara Hammond, for instance, a 17-year old general servant at the Royal Marine, had been born in Portsea, Hants, while Jesse Stephens, a still room maid at the hotel, was from Devonshire. Yet more interesting was the number of foreign nationals who also found employment in the local hotel and boarding house trade. The Royal Marine had a number of German and Belgian nationals as waiters and as porters. Henri Godfroid and Fredrick Batt, French and German nationals respectively, had positions as chefs de cuisine there. Several of the largest hotel establishments in Ventnor advertised to prospective clientèle that fluent French and German were spoken. There was clearly no better way to deliver this promise than by employing native speakers from the countries where those languages were used. The Royal Hotel, several hundred metres further west from the Royal Marine, appears to have had ten live-in servants in 1901 who were foreign nationals: seven from Germany, two from Switzerland and one from Austria. The hotel's chefs were, in turn, both from Switzerland.

Service staff at the Balmoral Hotel, western esplanade, Ventnor, circa 1900

When war broke out in Europe in August 1914, the local Ventnor newspaper was quick to record that the resort's many German waiters had nearly all left for home. Not only would they have become unwanted aliens if they had remained, but the clients that they had traditionally served would have ceased to visit anyway. German nationals, in particular, had often been among Ventnor's wealthiest visitors, entertained in the Ventnor Pavilion by German bands. Gertrude Cox, one of four sisters who holidayed in Ventnor in the final peacetime summer of 1913, left a vivid account of the cosmopolitan atmosphere that prevailed at the time. Together with their father, the sisters stayed at St. Augustine Villa, the iconic Swiss-Italianate building that still stands just west of the Cascade Gardens. The sisters could not fail to notice how there seemed to be a 'raid of foreigners' on the island that summer. Every second person they met, for example, was either French or German. The guests at the St. Augustine boarding establishment echoed the pattern: out of 19 individuals, there were seven different nationalities, and in a final twist, the boarding house itself was run by a family from Ireland.

Ventnor Bay around 1900

The guests at St. Augustine Villa would have looked out each day upon a beach lined not with fishing boats and fishing tackle but with wooden bathing machines, carefully segregated for men and for women. Tall striped canvas tents afforded further privacy for bathers and there were also ranks of deck chairs. Where boats could be observed drawn up on the beach, these were less for fishing than for taking visitors on pleasure trips out in Ventnor Bay or along other parts of the Undercliff coast. It was, nevertheless, the local fishermen who came to supply these various facilities, reinforcing the tradition of